BEING THERE

A COMPANION ON THE
PATHWAY OF ILLNESS

MARGARET T NAUGHTON

First published in 2016 by Messenger Publications

ISBN 978-1-910248-28-7

Designed by Messenger Publications Design Department
Typeset in Times New Roman and Nueva Std
Printed by Naas Printing Ltd

MESSENGER
PUBLICATIONS
JESUITS in IRELAND

Messenger Publications,
37 Lower Leeson Street, Dublin 2
www.messenger.ie

❧ INTRODUCTION ❧

We are all familiar with the cliché *health is wealth* but although most of us do from time to time utter this sentiment with genuine gratitude for our good health, it is usually only when we are faced with a deterioration in our physical or emotional well-being that we are forced to reflect on the importance of good health. For the majority of people, good health is a blessing granted and maintained for most of their life-time. However, for others, illness or ill-health can be a life-long affliction.

I work as a Healthcare Chaplain and I know from both personal and professional experience the impact of illness, sudden or more slow-burning, on one's life. The reality is that no one places illness on their wish list or Santa letter, but when it comes it is something that changes our lives. To lose control of our mind or body can be disabling and bewildering. Illness can rock us to the core of our being and drive us into a place of fear, loneliness and isolation. It can be difficult to find someone who can relate to our experience and listen to what's going on within our minds.

This book is an attempt to be a companion on the roadway of illness. It is a tool for both the person grappling with illness, and their loved ones, to try and make sense of illness and the impact it can have on our lives. This book could also serve as a guide for people working in the caring professions, a reminder that when people are sick their whole life has changed, and, as a result, they need patience, compassion and understanding from all around them. We can forget that the crankiness, impatience and sharp tongue are very often mask huge fear and anxiety.

For those struggling with illness, there will be questions about meaning, purpose and hope in life. There will be moments when the light becomes overwhelmed by the darkness of pain, fear and the unknown. There will be flashes of hopelessness and a multitude of questions, thoughts and considerations about ourselves, our families, our future and our God. Where is God in all of this?

For many, during these difficult days of pain and sickness, there can be either an absence or a sense of the presence of God. God can be at the centre of our experience or on the periphery of it. God can make himself known to us during these moments of darkness and hopelessness, or he can seem so very absent. During periods of illness, there can be doubts about our God, our faith and our value system. There can be flashes of deep, penetrating anger with God for letting us suffer. We can feel as Jesus felt in the garden when he begged and entreated his Father to take the cup of suffering from him, knowing that it was not to be.

The only way for Jesus was through his suffering and for those who travel the roadway of sickness and pain this too remains true of our experience. But, to walk through the fortress of physical, emotional or spiritual pain, demands courage and fortitude. It demands a person to be strong enough to face head on the pain of their condition and to open their hearts and souls to their Creator God.

When one is faced with the pain of life and of a crippling situation it can be so difficult to face the God of Job. This God is the god who oftentimes can seem to revel in our misery, to have closed his ear to our pleadings for healing, understand and fellowship. But there are times when the Jesus of the New Testament becomes apparent in our experience. This is the Jesus, as the gospels tell us, whose touch healed many. His words opened the ears and the eyes of many and brought hope and healing where it had long since been lost. This is the same Jesus who suffered and died on the Cross and who supports many of us when we carry the cross of ill health.

໑ LOSS ໑

In life we all experience many different losses. There can be the loss of a job, the failure to secure an expected result in an examination, the inability to become a parent, the loss of our beloved parent, spouse, sibling or friend. In fact, there is a myriad of different issues, which can be readily identified and accepted as being a loss. Illness is another type of loss, which we can face in our lifetime or someone we love can do so. It draws us into another world, another way of being. It takes us abruptly into a world of self-doubt, insecurity, fear, loss of control and certainty. It takes us by the hand and drags us violently into a sphere of the unknown. Illness destroys all that was certain for us. It shatters our equilibrium and ensures that our balance is mutilated. It disempowers us and puts us at the mercy of others. It means that all that was certain becomes anything but. It makes us dependent on others in a way we may never have been before. It is a loss that can cripple and paralyse. It can rob us of our hope, our light and our future. It can crumble the world that we have so carefully crafted, in which we are safe and secure. It can take us from the present moment of strength into a future of vulnerability and hopelessness.

Unlike the death of a loved one, illness is not always seen or acknowledged as a loss. It can be seen simply as something to get on with or get through.

But illness can and does impact upon us greatly. However, as each of us is unique in how we live our lives, so too are we individual in how we cope with illness, ill-health and well-being. Our personal reaction to our altered state of health can also be dependent on a number of factors such as severity of condition and long-term prognosis. But regardless of the condition or outlook, the loss of our physical, emotional or spiritual well-being even for a few days can be frightening, alien and life-altering. The loss of what was once so certain can catapult us into a realm of disbelief, unbelief and a gnawing fear that things will never be the same again. Indeed, in many ways, once we have journeyed through an illness or a period of prolonged ill-health, we are changed. We have walked the pathway of suffering and we have embraced that which is the weakest part of us. We have touched into our brokenness and have felt the pain deep within us. We have tapped into the vulnerability and fragility, which we all like to keep covered up and cut off. We have held loss in our hands in a way that has changed us. We have walked the Way of the Cross and we have had our pain and our fear illuminated by the light and hope of the Risen Lord. We have had our loss acknowledged and touched by the healing Jesus.

✷ HOSPITAL ✷

For many of us when we are faced with a new diagnosis or with a deterioration in our condition it is necessary for us to be admitted to hospital for assessment and/or treatment. I sense that no matter how often any of us find ourselves in a hospital, the reality of the experience remains very much unchanged. To be in a hospital can be a frightening and bewildering experience. All that was routine and normal for us is no more. All of a sudden a person finds themselves submerged into a world of technical language, charts, medication and often without warning or without transition. This can leave a person feeling threatened, isolated, vulnerable, frightened, immobilised in a way like never before. Very often people who in their regular, everyday jobs wear suits and assume significant levels of responsibility now find that they have been reduced to a pair of pyjamas, slippers and a medical diagnosis. They have become simply a number. They have become dehumanised, one in a long line of others waiting and hoping to be treated and sent home well again. Each person finds that they are now just one of many faceless individuals within a big and overcrowded system who find their world thrown into turmoil. Who are these people? What is their story? What pain do they carry deep within their souls? Who is the person beyond the diagnosis? Indeed, does anyone have the time or the energy to try and find out?

Who is there to listen to the experience of such an upheaval in daily routine? After all, in Western medicine, focus seems to lay totally in the curing of the ailment regardless of what the person themselves or their family want. As Thomas Moore has written:

> Modern medicine is hell-bent on cure. .. It wants to eradicate all anomalies before there is a chance to read them for their meaning. It abstracts the body into chemistries and anatomies so that the expressive body is hidden behind graphs, charts, numbers and diagrams.[1]

But hospitals are not populated by numbers or ailments. They are populated by men and women of different ages, classes, creeds and nationalities, who all have one thing in common – they are ill. However, besides being ill, these people are parents, siblings, neighbours and friends. They are important to those whom they love and who love them in return. Charles Vella, a hospital chaplain and priest who has written extensively on ethics in the service of the sick argues strongly that one's suffering is 'augmented by the humiliation of being thought of as a number on a bed, totally divested of their human dignity'.[2] And yet he believes the sick to be God's 'favourite children'[3], people with hearts and minds who, when in hospital, find themselves very often psychologically at rock bottom, immersed in a system that treats them very much as a number, an ailment, a diagnosis, an entity to cure. In recent times there has been a growing awareness of what's known as the biopsychosocial model of healthcare where it is recognised that a person is a totality of mind, body and spirit with a myriad of needs to be addressed during the hospital stay. There is recognition that the experience of being in hospital causes more than a physical upheaval to each person and their family but yet all the while we can find ourselves feeling lonely, desolate and misunderstood during a hospital admission. Despite the best attention of our healthcare workers, we can still feel overwhelmed by a system so alien and unknown to us. We can feel that we will never be the same again, that we will never get better, that tests will reveal bad or unexpected results, that we will walk out of the door of the hospital unable to cope with the news we have been given or the future that now awaits us. When we are sick or in hospital we are disempowered and thrown out of kilter and it is a frightening, bewildering experience. In fact, it can be one of the loneliest places to be despite all the noise and people that traverse its environs. The loneliness of hospital is akin to the desolation of Jesus in the Garden when he begged his Father to be with him in his suffering.

WHERE IS GOD IN ALL OF THIS?

This can be a lonely and desolate time. Being in hospital or the recognition that we need to be in hospital can arouse many different types of emotions in us. Spiritually we can find ourselves challenged like never before. We can feel like our God has abandoned us. It can seem that our illness is a punishment for something we didn't do right or for a previous or earlier wrong-doing. We can feel very angry with God or else we can start to bargain with him. We can beg and entreat him to take away our suffering, to give us good results, to make things better. We can promise or trade our future for good health. 'If only' becomes two magic words.

Despite the pain of uncertainty and the feeling that God is either absent or punishing us, He is there. He is walking that pathway of uncertainty and fear with us. He is carrying us and holding us as we journey very much into the unknown.

WHAT AM I TO DO?
THE PATIENT

Sometimes those around us can underestimate the impact being in hospital can and does have on us. There can be a sense of incredulity that we are feeling so anxious, so frightened and so uncertain. But the fear, the anxiety, the loneliness and the uncertainty are very real for you, so don't block them out. Acknowledge it, sit with it and allow yourself to feel the pain of your fear. There is no shame in being frightened in the hospital environment. There is no shame in feeling completely out of ones depth. There is no shame in feeling like one is swimming against the tide. After all, it is not the normal run of life to be ill. It is not something we wish for or at times understand. So allow yourself to be worried, or anxious or frightened. This is the pain that being a patient in a hospital can bring to us.

WHAT AM I TO DO?
THE COMPANION ON THE JOURNEY

When your friend or loved one is in hospital the greatest gift you can give them is your presence. Be there with love and understanding. Touch their fear and anxiety with love and compassion. You may not always comprehend what's going on for them or with them but do not turn away from them. In the midst of a world so alien and so frightening they need, in fact they crave, your normality, your presence, your love.

❧ ROUTINE ADMISSION ❧

The experience of hospital is above all one of uncertainty. It brings us into a world that we would much rather not have to embrace. Even when we know or have some time to become accustomed to the idea of going into hospital for a test or some routine procedure, there is still so much to fear or to be concerned about or with. In the days before we are admitted we can feel anxious and apprehensive. We do not know what way to turn or what avenue to walk. We can find it difficult to understand what is going on within us. We can feel cranky and full of fear. We can simply feel overwhelmed by the enormity of it all, the enormity of the unknown. We are aware that in a hospital nothing is certain and that there are risks attached to all procedures. We are fearful of the procedures, the tests and above all of the results. We are only too aware of the fact that people really don't know how to sit with our uncertainty or our fear.

People try to reassure us that all will be well but the reality is that these are false or misleading platitudes. There are no guarantees and nothing is or can be taken as a given. The reality of having to walk through the doors of a hospital and become little more than a number is disabling and dehumanising. It fills us with dread that the best words cannot really articulate. We are forced to inhabit a world where we lose our control. We lose our identity and we lose our certainty. We become pawns in a world that is not known or understood by most of us. We are manoeuvring within a world that we wish to run from. But our need to attend to the physical, emotional or spiritual aspect of our being means that we are waiting to walk into a world where we are simply another being, another person to cure, to fix, to make better. We are another man, woman or child who is filled with fear and trepidation in advance of an admission into hospital.

It may be routine, but there is nothing routine about our life when we walk through the doors of the hospital. There is nothing familiar anymore. We answer to the regime or regiment of another now. We have lost the power to make decisions about the simplest of things. Even our meal times are now at the mercy of others. This period is one of disconcertment and unknowing. It is a period when the light of hope becomes tainted by the darkness of the unknown.

WHERE IS GOD IN ALL OF THIS?

During these moments in advance of a hospital admission, God can feel so distant and so far away. He can feel like he has run away from us, abandoned us in our time of need. It can feel that he has let us down. We have prayed or asked that we won't have to be admitted to hospital and yet now we are faced with the reality that this cannot be avoided. We are coming face to face with a world that is full of sickness, death and dying and God has let us down. He is nowhere to be seen.

On the other hand, God can be so very near. We can sense him walking along this horrible pathway of uncertainty. We can feel his presence in the moments when we feel alone and not understood. We can become aware of his compassion and love when it seems not to be coming from others. In the loneliness and darkness of the unknown, we can be gifted the presence of the Companion God, the Jesus who walked the lonely road to Emmaus with his broken-hearted disciples in the aftermath of the crucifixion (Luke 24:13-49). We can hear the words 'Blessed are the poor in Spirit, theirs is the kingdom of God' (Matthew 5:3) ring loudly and clearly in our ears that hear little else but the beat of a fearful drum.

WHAT AM I TO DO?
THE PATIENT

Routine admissions to hospitals are planned and therefore there is time to mull over how we are feeling. Sometimes, this can be to our disadvantage in that we have time to think about the 'what ifs'. But having some time can also offer an opportunity for preparation for the admission both from a practical and an emotional perspective. During these moments of waiting, reach deep within and tap into the inner resources you have. Try to touch that place within that we all draw upon when times are tough or when we would rather run from the reality of our situation. Hold that in your thoughts and trust that you can and will be able to cope with what lays ahead of you. Trust in the strength that you carry with you always. You can survive what is ahead of you. You can cope with what you need to undergo. You can face into the pain of having to go into hospital. You can walk that roadway of fear with the knowledge that you have it within to see this challenge through.

WHAT AM I TO DO?
THE COMPANION ON THE JOURNEY

Be patient with your loved one. Support them during these anxious days of waiting. The worry that they have now is very real, very raw for them. They have many thoughts swirling around their heads and they are worried about what lies ahead. They need you to be strong enough to sit with that worry, that anxiety, that concern. They need a shoulder to lean on. They need the presence of someone who will not dictate, or judge or dominate. Be kind, be gentle, and be compassionate. Touch their pain with your fragility. Let your humanity touch theirs.

✎❧ UNEXPECTED ADMISSION TO HOSPITAL ❧✎

In many ways it is difficult to ascertain whether a scheduled or an unexpected admission to hospital is more difficult to deal with. When one is unexpectedly taken ill and when the illness or condition necessitates a hospital stay, people say that it feels like the bottom has fallen out of their world, that the parameters of their control have been segued. People speak of the anxiety and the fear, the deep-seated uncertainty. The suddenness and the shock of it all, the feelings such an unexpected admission can arouse are so disabling. The fear, the immediacy of it all is so alien, so frightening, so bewildering. When one hears of having to immediately make their way to the hospital, either themselves or with a loved one, it can feel like a dark cloud has moved over their head.

When one is asked to make their way to a hospital, they know not what lies ahead of them. If they have been asked to go to the local accident and emergency department there can be anxiety around how long they will be there for, who will they meet there, what will they be told, what tests will have to be done. It is not uncommon or obscure for questions to start swirling violently around and around in their head, whipping up a storm of fear and uncertainty. Such uncertainty, such darkness and such understandable fear around what the future could now hold for me, for us, for my family.

For a person who finds themselves within an accident and emergency department or a ward for the very first time, it can be very bewildering. Everything is so clinical, so big, so impersonal, so dehumanising. There is nothing comforting about this world. The fear is palpable; the heart-ache of many so real; the worry of what might be is tangible. The world of the hospital community for the person who walks it for the very first time can indeed make the heart and the soul heave in pain. It can crack open a shell of protection and make it crumble instantly. The person who is catapulted into this world unexpectedly for the first time is in a vulnerable and frightening place.

For a person who is somewhat more accustomed than the first time patient to being in hospital, there is still a myriad of emotions that become aroused when the realisation has dawned that they need to walk the hospital corridor once more. In many ways, the more regular service-user has a greater understanding of the hospital world, of the language, the routine, the structure but it is never an environment that becomes comfortable or sought out. For this person there is also the fear and the anxiety. There is the uncertainty and the loneliness. There is the deep-seated disappointment to have found that their condition has deteriorated once more and to such an extent that there is no other option but to be admitted to hospital. There is the knowing that their world is about to stop. There is the awareness that as the outside world continues to live and be and flourish that my world within the hospital community has now stopped. I am now frozen in time. I am living in a snapshot in time. As the birds continue to sing and the sun continues to shine, I am stuck here in a world of charts, technology and the unknown. There is the sheer frustration of having to grapple with a body or a mind that is ill. There is the sheer anger that this has happened to me again. There is the pain that this could be my life forever. There is the pain that my body or mind is not as strong as I need or would like it to be. There is the continuous pain that this could keep happening over and over again.

WHERE IS GOD IN ALL OF THIS?

In the pain and the uncertainty of it all, God is there. In our pain and frustration we are echoing the frustration of Mary and Martha when Jesus did not come on time to save their brother Lazurus. In this Gospel passage (John 11:1-45), we see the clear frustration of Mary and Martha whose hearts are broken at the death of their dear brother Lazurus. In the waiting and the torment of the sisters, there is the torment and the pain of anyone who finds themselves in hospital. Neither Mary or Martha, nor indeed Jesus, expected Lazurus to die. And when Jesus learned of the death of his friend he wept openly and with deep pain. His pain, his anger, his hurt and his frustration was so clear, so visible, and so very human. The Jesus who unexpectedly found himself weeping for his friend is the same Jesus who walks the journey with those of us who find ourselves in the place of unexpectedness. It is this same Jesus who knows, who understands and who feels our pain when we are engulfed by a torrent of fear and hopelessness when our life gets turned on its head by the unexpected hospitalisation of self or of someone whom we love.

WHAT AM I TO DO?
THE PATIENT

These are difficult days for you. The suddenness and the unexpectedness of the admission to hospital can create a feeling of fear and disempowerment. The not knowing, the hastiness of the admission, makes you feel out of control, out of your depth. Seek the support of someone whom you trust to share these thoughts and feelings. Seek out a family member, a friend, a hospital chaplain with whom you can be honest and open. Share your feelings with honesty. Don't run from the pain, the hurt, the fear, but instead find a safe and sacred space within which to share it. Do not carry the burden alone. Do not add another pain to your already long list of problems by struggling alone with the desolation of your situation. Share that brokenness with a safe pair of ears. Reach out longingly to someone whom you know is strong enough to hold your pain. Allow yourself to be touched by a healing and loving God.

WHAT AM I TO DO?
THE COMPANION ON THE JOURNEY

Do not be fearful of the uncertainty and the fear of your friend or loved ones during this time of their life. You must try to understand that their life has been turned upside down and they need you. You certainly can't change the reality of their situation but you can change one thing for them. You can help them to feel not alone but supported and loved. You can show them love and kindness and patience and let them know and feel that they are not alone. You can be the personification of the loving and healing Jesus by your very presence and patience and non-judgmental attitude. Let them be open and honest with you and do not dismiss or belittle their pain. They need you. They do not need false platitudes now but rather they need raw and real presence in their lives of someone who has no answers but who has the strength of character and depth of love to be with them in their pain.

❧ PRE-SURGERY ❧

One of the most invasive things that any of us will ever endure is to have surgery. It is something that disempowers us like nothing else. We are at the mercy and the skills of others who we hope and pray have the ability to do a good job. There is the knowing of what can go wrong and of how little we actually comprehend about the procedure we are about to undergo. There is the anxiety around speaking to the professionals about what is going to happen and equally what may go wrong. There is just an overwhelming fear of the whole process and the consequences for my future. There is the fear and worry and concern, not only of what could go wrong but also of the pain I will have to endure afterwards and for how long. There may be restrictions on driving; on working and on exercising in the aftermath of surgery, so there is much to take on board in the weeks and days before surgery. Surgery is a word we all like to run from. It is a word that conjures up butterflies in the tummy like nothing else. It is a word that whisks up an internal storm, a torrent of fire and hopelessness like never before. It is a disempowering, disabling, overwhelming word. No matter how many times one has surgery during their life there is always a fear that permeates the thoughts and the feelings in the run up to the procedure.

Depending on the type of surgery one is going for,

there may be a necessity to go into hospital a day or two beforehand for routine bloods and other tests to be done. These can also create feelings of uncertainty, confusion and anxiety adding to the already long list of emotions stirred up thanks to the impending surgery.

When one has to go into the hospital or healthcare facility on the morning of the procedure, this too creates its own problems and feelings. It is a long drive to the hospital knowing what is ahead during the day. It is a long morning of waiting, hoping and praying that all will work out. Anxious moments, anxious mornings during which one is completely disempowered by the not knowing, by the awareness that there is nothing we can do to quell the fear but rather that all that is left to do is to face into it.

WHERE IS GOD IN ALL OF THIS?

In the anxious, fear-filled hours and days ahead of surgery, God is there in the mess and the fear of it all. God is there shepherding us along the pathway. He is there helping us to hold on and be brave enough to face into the ordeal that lies ahead. In the gospels we read many times of the number of sick who ran to Jesus for healing – the blind, the deaf, the mute, those afflicted with venereal diseases. Jesus touched into their pain and healed them. He felt their pain and he listened to their pleas for healing. Jesus understood the physical and emotional pain of the sick and the afflicted. He cured many who had struggled for many years with their condition. He felt the hopelessness of their situation. Jesus could be said to have coined the concept of holistic care as he healed in more ways than one. This is the Jesus who is present to our emotional turmoil when we struggle and suffer and await the pain of something we would much rather run from. Jesus is in the difficult days of our waiting. But he is also in the joy of our relief when it is all over.

WHAT AM I TO DO?
THE PATIENT

It can be difficult to understand or express the anxiety that the word surgery conjures up for all of us. It is perfectly normal and natural to be fearful of surgery. It is absolutely understandable to want to cancel it or run away from it. But try not to let your fear and your anxiety overwhelm you. Sit with your fear and your sense of hopelessness. Do not block it out. Do not try to pretend that this is not happening. But instead, be honest with yourself and acknowledge that you are feeling apprehensive and concerned. Share these thoughts and feelings with someone whom you are confident can help you to face into this abyss of uncertainty. Trust that with the support of those around you that you will be able to undergo your procedure and not become overwhelmed by the 'what ifs'.

WHAT AM I TO DO?
THE COMPANION ON THE JOURNEY

A person facing surgery needs support and a conduit to express the deep inner turmoil that they have. They need a trusted ear to hear, to really hear their true and undiluted feelings around what they have to face. So do not be unwilling to be this ear. Give this person the greatest gifts of all, love and time.

POST-SURGERY

When we awake from surgery, there is firstly an overwhelming relief knowing that the surgery has been done and that we have come through it all. Then we may become aware of the physical pain, the grogginess from the medications and the noise of the recovery room. These are surreal moments in many ways as this is not a familiar territory and yet, there is a sense of relief to be there. There is still the journey to recovery to travel but intermingled within this there is the joy at being ready to face into the recovery period.

Depending on the procedure, and the severity of it all, the recovery period could vary from days to weeks, and in some cases, months. This means many alterations to our lifestyle and to our way of being. Again, dependent on our procedure, we may have to rely on others for assistance with the most basic of tasks, so this brings a certain amount of powerlessness and a degree of vulnerability.

For a person used to being in control, or being totally autonomous and independent, this can pose a bigger disruption to mind, body and soul than the surgery itself. These days can be quite emotional ones. We can feel many different emotions such as vulnerability, isolation, loneliness, dependence, fear, uncertainty and complete disempowerment. We can feel like we have lost control of our bodies and that we will never be the same again. There can be a further fear factor if tests had to be done during the surgery or if surgery was more extensive than first anticipated.

It is a lonely time, a time of spiritual, physical and emotional distress. It is like our lives have become frozen in time, a snapshot in time. The world goes on without us while we continue to exist but not to live. The walls outside of the hospital are full of life and hope, whereas for the recovering person the world can feel so devoid of both. We can long for hope but sometimes during these days we are unable to touch it, feel it or sense it.

WHERE IS GOD IN ALL OF THIS?

These are times of deep humility and disempowerment. These are days when we lose control of our lives. These are times when we feel disconnected from the world. No humbler image is there than the Son of God hanging on a Cross in Calvary, devoid of all his dignity and respect. And yet, it is when we are weak that we are strong. While on the Cross, Jesus is the strongest that He has ever been. In our times of struggle and humiliation we are the personification of the Suffering Jesus. It is when we struggle and suffer the humiliation of disempowerment that we are touched by the God who lost his life on the Cross for the world – battered and bruised by war, sin and division. It is this God who sits with us when we have no other companion.

WHAT AM I TO DO?
THE PATIENT

These can be dark and humiliating days. These are times of disconnectedness. But try not to allow yourself become disconnected. In the pain of what can be hopelessness and darkness, do not turn yourself away from those around you. Do not push away the fear and the physical and emotional pain you are feeling. Do not be ashamed by the physical, emotional and spiritual weakness you may now be feeling. Embrace it, feel it, touch it and hold it. Do not allow yourself to become buried underneath the weight that you are now carrying. Touch the feelings, the thoughts and the swirling moments of desolation with kindness, compassion and love for and to self.

WHAT AM I TO DO?
THE COMPANION ON THE JOURNEY

Try to be an understanding companion at this time. This can be a messy emotional and spiritual time for your beloved or friend. It can be a time of anger, hurt, resentment or incredulity. Be a loving and supportive ear for their wide spectrum of thoughts and feelings. Do not run away from them but rather stay the course and be the shoulder that they now lean on. Be that friend in a time of need.

✪ INTENSIVE CARE ✪

For those of us who find ourselves in an intensive care unit, the fear, terror and sense of vulnerability is heightened significantly. Here a person is subjected to an experience that can and very often does impact on the remainder of their lives. The sense of loneliness, abandonment, disempowerment and total dependency that can grip an ICU patient should never be underestimated. As an intensive care survivor myself, I am very much aware of the life-changing experience being so close to death can be. Not only is one close to death, but one is surrounded by death. Death, pain and suffering; loss and isolation permeate the environment of an intensive care unit. It can be such a lonely and desolate place to be; words uttered about your condition around you but never spoken directly to you; a reluctance to speak of the unspeakable possibility of one dying; sedated patients not spoken to but who can very often still hear but are unable to speak and are immobilised by both fear and isolation.

It is a reality that every day, in many different hospitals, people find themselves within the walls of an intensive care unit. For most, it is not a matter of routine, but usually as a consequence of a trauma or an emergency. Most people who end up in an intensive care unit are victims of an accident, a major cardiac or renal event, neurosurgery, an assault, respiratory issues, burns or a sudden and unexplained deterioration in one's physical health and well-being. For whatever reason, it is without doubt, certainly one of the most, if not the most frightening experience of one's life. To be well and suddenly and without warning end up in a place many only associate with death is unimaginably frightening. For others who assumed that they had been making significant progress and then without warning deteriorate to such an extent that intense medical treatment is needed immediately it is also a bewildering and terrorising place to find oneself.

The suddenness of it all can add significantly to the impact on the patient. For some patients, they are unable to recall much if anything about their stay in the ICU. However, having said that, not everyone responds to these experiences in the same way. For some, they are the making of character; for others its destruction.

I think that it is necessary that all this must be placed in context. For those of us working within a hospital environment, we can become accustomed to machinery, tubes, wires and so on. But for a person who knows very little about all this, an intensive care unit can appear to be very threatening. After all, there is a sense of being in an alien environment, where everything is strange, threatening almost. There are machines that make loud and strange noises. Indeed, sophisticated tools for coping with critically and seriously ill patients such as monitoring devices, an array of signal processors and reliable assessment displays, make the ICU the most technically advanced environment in a hospital. Nurses and Doctors alike receive advanced technical training so that they might monitor a patient's condition. This impressive array of complex equipment that surrounds the seriously ill patients, their relatives and staff members, allows Western medicine to take unprecedented care of the human body.

But, by its very nature, the intensive care unit is stressful and it is little wonder that patients complain of lack of privacy, being unable to sleep, bright lights, high noise levels. People also complain of enforced immobility, social isolation and communication problems.

The unit is also full of sick and dying people. Consequently, it is fair to say that death, pain and suffering permeate the air in such a place. It can be difficult not to lose heart in the face of such pain and suffering. Patients have often spoken of how difficult it is to stay positive when all around you continue to suffer. To move beyond this, there is also the overwhelming reality of being faced with one's own mortality. Possibly like never before has a person in an intensive care unit been faced with the reality that they are not immortal, that they will die like everyone else and very possibly much sooner that they had ever considered that they would.

It is a frightening place to find oneself and patients speak of a broad spectrum of feelings whilst there. Fear is possibly one of the biggest feelings spoken about amongst patients with regard to a time spent in an intensive care unit. Fear of the unknown, fear of being in an incomprehensible environment and the ambiguity of being an object of clinical vigilance is very real. There is also the deep sense of isolation, of being alone, of being invisible as a person. One is very much a stranger being cared for by another stranger. One becomes totally and completely disempowered, at the mercy of someone else to look after one's basic and fundamental needs. One is not only at the mercy of another human being to tend to their needs but also highly dependent on machinery to keep them alive. Everything that was normal is gone. The shock one feels at finding themselves as helpless as a newborn baby can be overwhelming.

Difficulties around communicating also arise. Often ventilated and sedated there is an assumption made by medical and non-medical staff alike that patients are unable to hear. Very often patients can hear but are unable to speak. That huge lack of ability to communicate can be quite soul destroying.

It is a reality that every serious illness or injury is a threat to life. Therefore, whether a patient is aware of it or not, a stay in an intensive care unit represents a dance with death. Whether one likes it or not, here, in the ICU a person comes face to face with ones own mortality. No matter how weak or vulnerable a patient may feel they fight on, faced with the reality that their fight may be futile but so very often the human will to survive raises its head and in spite of an unnerving insecurity and uncertainty the human instinct is to fight. It is often when one is confronted with the reality of death that the value of life emerges. However, it is also difficult to be surrounded by that desperate fight for life. Patients speak of being frightened and unnerved by being surrounded by death. This is a particularly painful experience for elderly or long-term patients of an intensive care unit.

Another implication for patients while in or shortly after leaving the ICU involves the whole psychological-existential realm. Put more simply, I refer to this as the 'why' questions. What is the meaning of my life? What is it all about? Why am I here? Why did this happen to me? Why do I have to suffer? Where do I go to from here? Will I get another chance? Will I get time to put things right with my family? What does my future hold? These types of questions emerge from people with or without a belief system. When one is standing on the threshold of life and death, one becomes aware of the need to assess one's life and indeed ones future. So often patients have spoken of regrets, broken promises, guilt, shame and are apprehensive but welcoming of the opportunity for more time to mend what is or has been broken. Moreover, patients are given a chance to assess why they work as hard as they do and ask is the striving for money and success so important now? What is the thing that gives them most meaning in life? A confrontation with death opens up many existential questions while there is still time to try and answer them. It offers the opportunity to re-evaluate one's life and perhaps of a hopeful future that past wrongs can be put right.

It is important to remember that for every person who finds themselves in an ICU there are also family members who are affected by the experience. Just as the patient has been plunged into chaos, so too has the person's family. They too become caught up in the alien and technical environment, which is new and threatening to them. And one must remember it is a place they did not expect to find themselves in. They want to help their loved one but are unsure what to do or what to say. They too have been faced with the gravity of the situation and they speak of desperation and powerlessness as well as fear of the unknown.

WHERE IS GOD IN ALL OF THIS?

It can be difficult to see God in a place like an ICU. It can be impossible to believe that God could exist within the walls of such an environment. It is challenging to find God, see him or sense his presence in the midst of such darkness and pain. It can be so damn hard to think that there is anything or anyone beyond the chaos of the here and now of the ICU. But one is not forgotten by God in here. God, the Good Shepherd is close at hand. Like the shepherd who left behind his ninety-nine sheep to seek out and find his one lost sheep, so too does God seek out, find and hold the suffering person in the ICU (Luke 15: 4-7). You are not alone, remember God is with us always, yes to the end of time (Matthew 28:20).

WHAT AM I TO DO?
THE PATIENT

Remember that you are a vulnerable, fragile and human individual. The time spent in an ICU can be overwhelming. Embrace your fragility during this time. Let not your physical or emotional brokenness overwhelm you or disempower you. Allow yourself to feel and sense and know that this is an alien environment. Allow yourself to be aware that within such an environment is death and illness and uncertainty like in no other area of a hospital. It is alright to be frightened and it is perfectly normal to be bewildered and disempowered. Do not be hard on yourself for feeling out of your depth. Accept that there is nothing normal or usual about this place. There is nothing to be ashamed of when we say that we simply do not want to be here, that we would rather run from here than stay. In the safety of such an alien world, there is a duality between life and death, between hope and hopelessness, light and darkness.

WHAT AM I TO DO?
THE COMPANION ON THE JOURNEY

If your loved one is in an ICU they are in a world that is most likely also alien to you. Share your concerns with staff if you feel that you are finding the environment challenging or overwhelming. There is no shame in admitting that you feel somewhat uneasy within such a world. Your loved one needs you to be there for them. They need you to be able to support them through a very difficult time for them. Be honest with them at all times about what you know regarding their situation. Support them and let them have space and scope to say how they are feeling. Do not brush away their fears because you may feel a little ill at ease in such a place. They need the truth. They need reality. They need humanity from you. So open your hearts and souls to them and let them be free in how they express their feelings. Be strong and yet be vulnerable. Be hopeful and hope-filled. Be broken and be whole. Be a symbol of normality in a world that is anything but. Be a companion to someone who very much needs a smile, a word, a person who can be a rock of calm in the midst of a storm.

RECUPERATION PERIOD/ POST-HOSPITAL PERIOD

It is interesting how although none of us wish to be in a hospital, nevertheless, when we are discharged, it can be quite difficult to readjust to normal life and our usual environment and routine. Ironically, despite the uncertainty, the fear the not knowing night from day sometimes, there is at the same time, a certain degree of safety for us in being in hospital. This is in the sense that we have company all the time, medical treatments onsite twenty-four hours a day and a deep awareness that we are understood within this world. When we come home, very often our families can't connect with our experience, nor are they able to sit with our feelings around what has just happened for us. There can be the desire to speak of our experience but we are met only with silence, a wall of silence. Words can be spoken to us that alienate us from our experience. People tell us how lucky we are to be alive, to be getting better, to be home but sometimes we just need someone to listen to us and sit with our thoughts on what has been. There can so be a need to have someone affirm that what we have gone through has been difficult and that time will be needed for holistic healing to happen.

These are alienating days. These are days of reflection, recollection and readjustment. These are days when patience, friendship, fellowship, and the extended hand is needed and sought and hoped for.

WHERE IS GOD IN ALL OF THIS?

Jesus spent forty days in the desert. These were difficult days. These were days of personal pain and reflection. These were days spent in isolation, away from the world and from those whom he loved far from home, locked in a world not known or understood by anyone. When we are recuperating or trying to make sense of the experience of hospital, illness, death, dying, mortality we are in our desert. We are in a place where it can be difficult to be found, and even more difficult to be touched. We are changed, we are different, and we are not as we once were. We are seeking to be reached but we can be hard to find. We can be in our desert of pain and isolation like Jesus was. We are sitting with Jesus and He with us in the desert of the long moments, the endless days when time seems to stand still for me but continues to move for others. He is there in the minutes, hours and days of being untouchable in our grief for what has recently visited our door.

WHAT AM I TO DO?
THE PATIENT

Allow yourself to sit with the isolation, the vulnerability and the restlessness. Do not be a harsh self-critic or condemn yourself for feeling so ill at ease in your world of normality. Illness and hospitalisation is a life-altering experience. It is a journey into a world without borders or indeed without rules. Having survived the experience, we feel out of synch. We can feel like a person in no man's land. We have one foot in our old world while another remains in the new world of the hospital. While we have eagerly awaited recuperation time or home time, it can be so difficult to find our place back in our old world. We have changed. Our illness has changed us and we can find it so very difficult to walk our old pathway once more. It is a period of restlessness. It is a period of growing and a period of change. It is a time of anxiety but also a time of hope. Do not be afraid of these changes. Do not feel like we have to be as we once were. The reality is that you will never again be the person you once were. Sit with that. Embrace that. Be the new me. Let not the expectations of self and of others thwart the journey for you now. Do not isolate yourself. Be a friend to self and allow others to be your friend.

WHAT AM I TO DO?
THE COMPANION ON THE JOURNEY

There can be a tendency by a person to isolate themselves during the recuperation period. They can feel ill at ease with self and with the world so oftentimes people struggle with low mood or isolation. There can be a feel of being an alien in their old world. There can be a sense that they are now strangers in their own world. Do not let a person struggle alone. Acknowledge that their experience has changed them but also realise that they are still your loved one or friend. They still need you. They still need you to reach out and be there for them. So do not run. Do not let them alone to struggle with their fears and their desolation. Embrace them and their vulnerability. Be not afraid to open your heart to them and to their pain. Be a safe space for the pain and the vulnerability to be exposed.

⤜ THE ELDERLY ⤛
AND THE MOVEMENT TOWARDS OLD AGE AND
LONG-TERM INFIRMITY

Most of us spend very little time thinking about growing old. In the hustle and bustle of life, we simply get on with things. We move from day to day, week to week, event to event and old age seems so very distant. Old age is something that belongs only to our parents or grandparents. We have so many milestones to reach that we strive day after day to get to them and to chase the next one that before we know it we have become our parents and then, our grandparents.

Old age brings with it an array of joys but it also presents many challenges and difficulties. Much of my daily work is done with older people. These are people who have reached many decades and are coming to the end of their days. Many of these people have lived full and happy lives and now have grandchildren, and even great-grandchildren around them. They speak to me, the chaplain, of the many things they have seen and the many changes their generation have borne witness to.

Old age is a time when people reflect on what has been, what might have been, what was good and what was challenging about life. It is also a period of time when questions are asked around meaning and purpose. Many people find themselves asking internally and externally what has their life been about. What have they achieved? Why couldn't things have been different?

When older people find themselves sick and in hospital they are in a particularly vulnerable position. They are faced with the reality of life and death, health and illness, healing and sickness.

For an older person who has always been so independent, it can be heart-breaking to find oneself in hospital perhaps for the first time. It can be such a big change for someone who has been exposed to little if any personal or familiar sickness to now being at the mercy of others for assistance with the basic needs and necessities of life.

Older people speak of the vulnerability aging brings. They speak of the swiftness of the years passing. They speak of the dreams unlived and the stories untold. While in hospital and sick, the elderly find time for reflection, regret, renaissance and renewal.

For family members it can also be somewhat challenging to see a mother or a father who was once so strong and so independent now disempowered and dependent on them and others for help. Old age can be such a lonely and desolate time. Old age can be a time of such isolation and fear. It can be a time when we become overshadowed by the fear and the uncertainty of the future.

For older people, a big concern is about health, independence and survival. Many times I have sat with an older person who is now either too ill or too frightened to live on their own. There is now no other option for them but to go and live in a nursing home or other healthcare facility.

This is one of the most difficult decisions people may find themselves faced with. It is such a huge step to leave all that was and is familiar and go to live in a nursing home. People end up leaving their home, their belongings, their routine, their friends, their neighbours, indeed their whole life to begin again in a world they usually do not really wish or want to embrace.

For people who need to make this decision, they need love, compassion and space to speak their mind. They need time and opportunity to express the losses such a big move brings and the fear and anxiety brought on by such a massive change. They need to be touched gently and respectfully by the world they have so lovingly helped to create for us and for those who will walk it after us. We need to respect and hold the pain of our beloved parents and grandparents whose lives are shaped now not by beauty and strength and youth but rather by fragility, delicacy and age.

WHERE IS GOD IN ALL OF THIS?

When we think of old age in many respects we are thinking of and paying homage to the vulnerability of the human state. We are vulnerable many times in our lives but especially so when we are old and sick. When Mary, the mother of Jesus sat at the foot of the Cross on Good Friday her heart and soul heaved in pain at the sight of her beloved son, dying so needlessly and so cruelly. In many ways, old age seems to personify such cruelty. It is cruel and unfair to be sick, as it is to grow old. When Jesus made his disciple responsible for Mary his mother after his death on the Cross, he was preparing for her vulnerability (John 19:26). He was ensuring that she had someone in her life during her old age and possible infirmity that would look after her when he was gone. The compassionate and caring Jesus was touching into the pain of his mother, into the pain of her future, without her son, that was so uncertain.

God is in all that we do. He is in all our struggles. In the vulnerability of old age and infirmity He is there holding us in the palm of his hand. He is helping us and reaching out to us in a way like no one else can. He is the rock that will support us in the darkness of uncertainty and the unknown.

WHAT AM I TO DO?
THE PATIENT

Be proud of who you are. Be proud of what you have done with your life, no matter how insignificant you may feel that your life has been, it has been a celebration of the person who you are today. Be open to sharing your experiences with those around you, young and old alike. When you are sad and feeling vulnerable, do not feel that it is a broken part of you, instead see it and believe it to be your greatest gift to the world.

WHAT AM I TO DO?
THE COMPANION ON THE JOURNEY

Old age is something we can find somewhat difficult to face. There is a reticence to sit with those who are nearing the end of their lives. In a world that celebrates beauty and majesty, old age can be a very visible opposite to this. But the reality is that old age, while having many challenges and difficulties, is a gift denied to many. So do not run from those around you who are silver-haired and in the eyes of the world old and perhaps infirm. When you look into their eyes see not weakness but rather allow yourself to see the strength that is within them. These are eyes that have seen many changes in life and have shed many tears. These are eyes that have seen the wrongs within our world and have tried to do something to change very many of them. Give of your time to those whose time in this world has helped to shape the world for us and for the future generations to come. Lend a shoulder to those whose hard work has built the foundation of the world as we now know it. Do not allow infirmity, grey hair and wrinkles thwart your vision. Do not allow these to block your eyes from seeing the true value of their life and when you allow yourself to see the value of he or she sitting in front of you, you are finally meeting your incarnate God.

PERSONAL DARKNESS

There are many different ways of struggling with ill-health. We can suffer physical, emotional or spiritual sickness. When we have a visible, tangible sign of illness we can be the recipients of love, compassion, empathy and patience. However, when we struggle with an illness that is invisible to the naked eye, there can be less empathy for us. There is less acceptance or tolerance for the battle waging within us.

People struggle to comprehend the pain of a person struggling with personal darkness. It can be so difficult to understand the pain of someone who feels overwhelmed by the loneliness and desolation of life and of their illness. This is a type of ill-health that is beyond the comprehension of many.

When we struggle with our emotions, we can feel so out of sync, so out of touch with the world and those around us. When our day-to-day living becomes engulfed by a cloud of darkness, we struggle and we struggle badly. We see nothing but a dark hole, an empty abyss of nothingness. It is a heavy cross to carry. The pain of emotional sickness is gut-wrenching. It is shattering.

When we struggle with our emotional well-being, we do not know where to turn or who to turn to. The pain of life can become just too much to bear. It is a pain, though not visible, that is so penetrating that it cuts through our mind, body and soul.

When we find ourselves cut off in pain from life and from the world, we are desolate and alone. Life has lost its colour, its meaning, its vibrancy. There is no light, no hope, no taste for that which is good within us and beyond us. There is a heavy rock of pain and anxiety deep within us. We are cocooned in a world that is safe and yet disempowering. We are situated in a world where although we are living as far as those around us can see, in actual fact, we are only existing, pained by the deep pain within us. We are pained very often by what others don't see. We are pained by that which we shield others from.

There is a cloud of fear and isolation and deep anxiety, which a struggle with darkness or depression, or whatever we chose to call it, brings. It is the deep, deep pain of desolation. It is the deep fear of being along, of feeling alone, of wanting to connect but of also wanting to disconnect. It is the pain that comes from life. It is the pain of hurt, loss, desolation and separation. It is the pain of one hurting like never before. It is the pain that echoes that of Jesus on the Cross: 'My God, my God, why have you forsaken me?'

WHERE IS GOD IN ALL OF THIS?

A person struggling with emotional well-being is someone who is loved and honoured by God. A person who feels overwhelmed by a personal cloud of darkness is held by the God who held his apostles when they too felt alone and unloved and unsupported. In his time of fear, Peter denied Jesus three times and yet he was forgiven and he was loved (Luke 22: 54-65). When we struggle with our emotions, with our fragility and our humanity we are the frightened Peter who is gripped by anxiety and doubt. We are the broken Peter who cries out in fear to a God who loves him. Our God is Peter's God who loves us and supports us no matter what. Our God is He who supports each and every one of us even when we think we are alone. In the fear of the unknown, in the fear of life, we are held. God is holding us and carrying us, bringing us safely home.

WHAT AM I TO DO?
THE PATIENT

Even though you now struggle, remember that you are not alone. Remember that there is a world around you that you are part of. Do not isolate yourself from those around you, even though sometimes it might seem like a better, safer option. Try not to let your darkness overwhelm you. Feel the fear within you, hold, embrace it and let it go. It is very hard to struggle with personal darkness. It is a horrible cross to carry. It is a curse that can blight your life. But trust in your own value as a human being. Trust that you are loved and valued by the world. Trust that you have inner resources that will see you through these dark and difficult moments. Seek the help and support of those around you. At first they may be uneasy. This may be because they are unsure how to support you or what to say. But do not let awkwardness or unease be a barrier between you and a world that cares for you. Reach out to the world and it will touch you back. In the loneliness of the darkness, the flickering light of hope will find a way of shining.

WHAT AM I TO DO?
THE COMPANION ON THE JOURNEY

Please do not run from the messiness and the brokenness that is personal darkness. When a person is struggling, they need your presence, your strength, your hope and your light. They may not be able to find these resources within themselves but be that foundation stone of a new beginning for them. Be that light of hope that they need to have the courage to face into the future. Be a beacon, a tower of strength for them. Even when you think you are too weak, too vulnerable, too whatever to be of help to them – stay the course and be there. You can be the best tool ever in their road towards recovery, on their road to a better tomorrow. Just be you. Just be there. And just be a friend who has no agenda, no rules, no demands. Just be the light that will guide them home on a stormy night.

✎ CONCLUSION ✎

Illness is a heavy cross to carry. We can suffer in so many ways and in so many situations. Our illness can be short-lived or more chronic, but it changes us. Illness always changes us. It redefines our parameters and makes us re-think many things in our lives. Illness can bring about new beginnings or it can close off many of our hopes and dreams. When we are sick we need love, comfort, support and strength from those around us. When we are unwell we need to be touched by the love of our family and friends. When we are ill we need our physical, emotional and spiritual brokenness to be touched, held and healed by God our Father. We need the love of the incarnate Son who died on the Cross for us to bind up our broken hearts and heal our wounds. We need the human love of a Divine God to touch our lives. We need the courage and the fortitude to walk forward and to be able to begin anew. Our life has changed, not ended. We need to feel the hand of the Companion God in ours as we walk into a future often filled with uncertainty and fear, because in his hand, ours will be forever safe.

PRAYERS
AND WORDS
OF COMFORT

FOR WHEN WE ARE ILL OR THOSE AROUND US ARE ILL

෨ඐ PSALM 4: 2, 4

When I call, answer me, O God of justice;
From anguish you released me, have mercy and hear me.
It is the Lord who grants favours to those whom he loves;
The Lord hears me whenever I call him

෨ඐ PSALM 5

To my words give ear O Lord
Give heed to my groaning
Attend to the sound of my cries
My King, my God

෨ඐ PSALM 9:10,14

For the oppressed let the Lord be a stronghold
A stronghold in times of distress
Those who know your name will trust you
You will never forsake those who seek you
Have pity on me Lord see my sufferings
You who save me from the gates of death
That I may recount all your praise.

෨ඐ PSALM 18: 2

God is my rock and my fortress
My deliverer is my God
I take refuge in him, my rock,
My shield, my saving strength
My stronghold, my place of refuge.

෨ඐ PSALM 18: 6

I cried to God in my anguish
I cried for help to my God
From his Temple he heard my voice,
My cry came to his ears.

There is a season for everything, a time for every occupation
    under heaven:
A time for giving birth,
A time for dying;
A time for planting,
A time for uprooting what has been planted.
A time for killing,
 A time for healing;
A time for knocking down,
A time for building.
A time for tears,
A time for laughter;
A time for mourning,
 A time for dancing.
A time for throwing stones away,
A time for gathering them;
A time for embracing,
A time to refrain from embracing.
A time for searching,
A time for losing;
A time for keeping,
A time for discarding.
A time for tearing,
A time for sewing;
A time for keeping silent,
A time for speaking.
A time for loving,
A time for hating;
A time for war,
A time for peace.

✒ PSALM 22

The Lord is my Shepherd,
There is nothing I shall want.
Fresh and green are the pastures where he gives me repose.
Near restful waters he leads me to revive my drooping spirit
He guides me along the right path, he is true to his name.
If I were to walk in the valley of darkness, no evil would I fear
For you are there, with your crook and with your staff and
*   with these you give me comfort.*

✒ MATTHEW 5: 3-10

How blessed are the poor in spirit:
The kingdom of heaven is theirs.
Blessed are the gentle:
They shall have the earth as their inheritance.
Blessed are those who mourn:
They shall be comforted.
Blessed are those who hunger and thirst for righteousness:
They shall have their fill.
Blessed are the merciful:
They shall have mercy shown them.
Blessed are the pure in heart:
They shall see God.
Blessed are the peacemakers:
They shall be recognised as children of God.
Blessed are those who are persecuted in the cause of right:
The kingdom of heaven is theirs.

✒ MATTHEW 6: 25-29, 34

That is why I am telling you not to worry about your life and
what you are to eat, nor about your body and how you are to
clothe it. Surely life means more than food, and the body more
than clothing. Look at the birds in the sky. They do not sow
or reap or gather into barns; yet your heavenly Father feeds
them. Are you not worth much more than they are? Can any

of you, for all his worrying, add one single cubit to his span of life? And why worry about clothing? Think of the flowers growing in the fields; they never have to work or spin; yet I assure you that not even Solomon in all his regalia was robed like one of these. So do not worry about tomorrow; tomorrow will take care of itself. Each day has enough trouble of its own.

✂ MATTHEW 7: 7-8
Ask, and it will be given to you; search and you will find; knock and the door will be opened to you. For the one who asks always receives; the one who searches always finds; the one who knocks will always have the door opened to him.

✂ MATTHEW 6: 5-13
And when you pray, do not imitate the hypocrites; they love to say their prayers standing up in the synagogues and at the street corners for people to see them. I tell you most solemnly, they have had their reward. But when you pray, go to your private room and, when you have shut your door, pray to your Father who is in that secret place, and your Father who sees all that is done in secret will reward you.

In your prayers do not babble like the pagans do, for they think by using many words they will make themselves heard. Do not be like them; your Father knows what you need before you ask him. So you should pray like this: Our Father in heaven, may your name be held holy, your kingdom come, your will be done, on earth as in heaven. Give us today our daily bread. And forgive us our debts, as we have forgiven those who are in debt to us. And do not put us to the test, but save us from the evil one.

✂ MATTHEW 26:36-39
Then Jesus came with them to a plot of land called Gethsemane; and he said to his disciples, 'stay here while I go over there to pray.' He took Peter and the two sons of

Zebedee with him. And he began to feel sadness and anguish. Then he said to them, 'My soul is sorrowful to the point of death.' Wait here and stay awake with me. And going on a little further he fell on his face and prayed. 'My father' he said, 'if it is possible, let this cup pass by me.' Nevertheless let it be as you, not I, would have it.

◈ MARK 1: 32-34
That evening, after sunset, they brought to him all who were sick and those who were possessed by devils. The whole town came crowding round the door, and he cured many who were suffering from diseases of one kind or another. He also cast out many devils, but he would not allow them to speak, because they knew who he was.

◈ MARK 6: 53-56
Having made the crossing, they came to land at Gennesaret and tied up. No sooner had they stepped out of the boat than people recognised him, and started hurrying all through the countryside and brought the sick on stretchers to wherever they heard he was. And wherever he went, to village, or town, or farm, they laid down the sick in the open spaces, begging him to let them touch even the fringe of his cloak. And all those who touched him were cured.

◈ LUKE 4: 40-41
At sunset all those who had friends suffering from diseases of one kind or another brought them to him, and laying his hands on each he cured them. Devils too came out of many people, howling, 'you are the son of God'. But he rebuked them and would not allow them to speak because they knew that he was the Christ.

REFLECTIVE PRAYER

THESE PRAYERS CAN BE USED AS REFLECTIVE PIECES,
PERSONAL PRAYERS OR INTERCESSORY PRAYERS

When we struggle in mind, body or soul, we need the healing touch of the Lord our God in our lives. We pray that we may always be aware of his presence in our lives.

Illness rocks us to the core of our being. We pray for the intercession of the Lord during these dark moments in our lives and that our pain will be touched by his healing and compassion.

When we are desolate and alone, we need the support of a God who cares more than we can ever know.

The prophet Jeremiah assures us that before we were formed in the womb God knew us and loved us. When we are ill or feeling down in ourselves, we long for the love and the compassion of our Creator God. May we never feel alienated from him or his love.

In the outstretched arm of our God we find love, compassion and support in times of trouble and strife.

When I fall, like Jesus did three times, may God pick me up, hold me, and carry me and bring me safely home.

In the brokenness of life, may I always find hope, light and meaning in those who empower me to continue on my journey when I struggle and fall.

May the God who sought out his one lost sheep always hold us and carry us when we have no fight left within us. May our brokenness be touched by his healing power.

When life is not good, we can feel so disconnected from God and from those around us. In such times, may the presence of God in the mess of it all, be revealed in the smallest of ways.

Healing comes in so many ways – in a smile, in an outbreak of laughter, in the offer of a meal or a drive. May we always recognise these small gifts as the personification of the God who loves us more than we can ever know or hope to understand.

In the palm of his hand, God holds all those who are dear to him.

In the palm of his hand, God carries the troubles of a broken world.

In the pain of today, we find the strength to face a new tomorrow.

May the God who created us hold us and heal us when life seems dark and destructive.

When my cloud of darkness fails to lift, may God raise me high so that I will now see only light, hope and love.

The pain of illness is a deep, penetrating one. When we struggle we feel alienated from our God and from those around us. Please God, never leave us stuck in that horrible place, feeling lost and alone.

(Endnotes)

1 Thomas Moore, *Care of the Soul: A Guide for Cultivating Depth and Sacredness in Everyday Life* (London: Harper, 1992) p155

2 Charles Vella, *Ethics in the Service of the Sick* (Dublin: Veritas, 2009) p17

3 Vella, p18

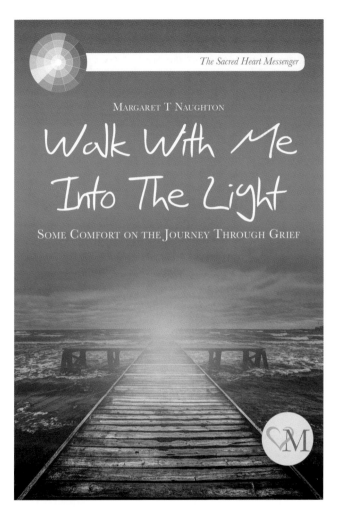

The Sacred Heart Messenger

Margaret T Naughton

Walk With Me Into The Light

Some Comfort on the Journey Through Grief

€3.99
WWW.MESSENGER.IE
TEL: 01-7758522

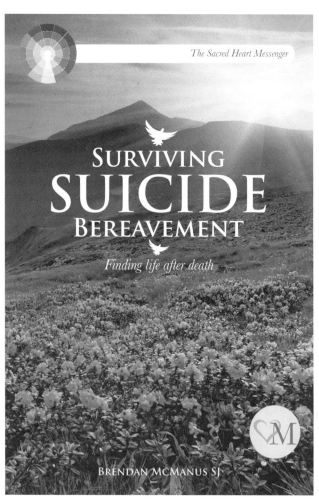

The Sacred Heart Messenger

Surviving
SUICIDE
Bereavement

Finding life after death

Brendan McManus SJ

IGNATIAN BOOKSHOP

€3.99
WWW.MESSENGER.IE
TEL: 01-7758522